Inclusive Classroom Activities
to promote
Social Interaction
and
Critical Thinking

RIDDLED
with
RIDDLES

2nd Edition

Melinda E. Clougherty, MS-CCC

Grades 3-6

TABLE OF CONTENTS

THE RIDDLES GAME

GAME COMPONENTS

A reproducible manual of riddles and their answers on an 8 x 10 inch format with cutting lines provided.

Variations of play; whole classroom activity (22 or more children)

Small therapy group (3-6 players)

WHOLE CLASSROOM ACTIVITY
RIDDLE HUNT

Prep; copy as many riddles as needed for the size of the classroom. Cut the riddles and answers into separate pieces. For example, 11 riddles/answers would be needed for a classroom of 22 students.

Divide the students into two groups. Seat the students from group A at tables or place them in a stationary position around the classroom. Give each of them the answer to a riddle. Give a set of riddle clues to each of the students in Group B. Tell them the object of the game is to "find their partner" by going around to one student from Group A at a time, read them the clues and confer with them to decide if it's a match. These riddles were designed to be unsolvable by themselves i.e. you must go "find your partner" in order to solve the riddle.

RIDDLE SPLASH

Use the Riddle Splash template to create a nice lesson plan with more linguistic support for your more challenged students. Xerox one copy of the Riddle Splash template. Choose a set of riddles and write the answers on the riddle splash. Xerox a copy of the riddle splash and give one to each student. All students remain seated. The teacher/therapist reads one set of clues and challenges a student to identify the answer to the riddle. "Why do you think it's the _____?" will help the student practice their ability to explain an answer.

RIDDLE LINE UP

Here is another fun variation to the game. Choose ten students to stand at the front of the class. Give them each an answer to the riddle. Ask them to read the answer to the rest of the class and display it so the other students can see it. Give each seated student a set of clues. Ask one student to read their set of clues out loud for the rest of the class to hear. Challenge them to identify the matching answer from the students standing in the front of the class.

SMALL GROUP PLAY

In a small group, give each student five answers to the riddles. They can either hold them in their hands or place them face up on the table. The teacher/therapist reads the clues to a riddle from the manual. The player who has the correct answer to the riddle gets credit for that round of play and spins a spinner to collect points.

RIDDLE SLAP

For a slightly more competitive variation of play, the teacher/therapist places numerous riddle answers in the middle of the table. She reads a set of clues. The first player to "slap" the correct answer to the riddle wins a point.

RIDDLE SPLASH ON A WHITE BOARD

The teacher writes the answers to ten riddles on the Smart Board or white board as well as the clues to one riddle. The students take turns crossing out possible answers by process of elimination until they arrive at the answer to the riddle. For example, "I know it's not the suitcase because…. Or I know it's not the the chestnut because….. I think it's the hearing aid because it requires a battery."

LITERACY CENTER
RIDDLE MATCH

While you run a reading group, you can keep a diverse set of students occupied. Cut up a set of riddle clues and answers. Challenge the students to match them up using their critical thinking skills, group discussion, process of elimination or by saving the hardest one for last etc.

WRITING EXTENSION ACTIVITY

Would you like to make a prediction about the answer to your riddle? _____

_____

_____

Why do you think so? _____   _____

_____

_____

PAIR SHARE QUESTIONS

What surprised you about your riddle and its answer? _____

_____

_____

What was funny about your riddle?_____

_____

_____

What did you learn from your riddle? _____

_____

_____

Can you improve upon this riddle? Can you rewrite a clue? Can you make it funnier or less obvious? _____

_____

_____

RIDDLE SPLASH

1 _____

2 _____

3 _____

4 _____

5 _____

6 _____

7 _____

8 _____

9 _____

10 _____

11 _____

12 _____

13 _____

14 _____

15 _____

16 _____

17 _____

18 _____

19 _____

20 _____

1) Some people lie about it. 2) Some people brag about it. 3) It changes over time.	Your age
1) Everybody has them. 2) Some people try to get rid of them. 3) Most people accept them.	Wrinkles
1) It is usually a rude thing to do. 2) It is usually involuntary. 3) It happens for a reason.	A burp
1) Some people have had many. 2) Some people have only had a few. 3) You can't choose it.	A birthday
1) It is usually expensive. 2) It usually involves many people. 3) It is always exciting.	A wedding

1) Every baby has one. **2)** It can be copied. **3)** It can be folded.	A birth certificate
1) You don't see one everyday. **2)** Part of it can make music. **3)** It is always found outside.	A parade
1) It can be cut in different styles. **2)** It can be cheap or expensive. **3)** It requires a tip.	A haircut
1) They require a lot of attention. **2)** People enjoy watching them. **3)** You can see them at the park.	A baby
1) This person works near a body of water. **2)** They are usually sedentary. **3)** They can be a hero.	A lifeguard

1) It can be long or short. 2) People perform to receive it. 3) It is usually done by a group of people.	Applause
1) You can live without one. 2) It has a door that opens. 3) You can't find it in the living room.	A dishwasher
1) It has two pieces. 2) It wouldn't look good on a hippo. 3) Older people usually don't wear one.	A bikini
1) It can be placed anywhere on the body. 2) It is hard to remove. 3) It is a form of art.	A tattoo
1) You don't see it very often. 2) Leprechauns like it. 3) It doesn't last very long.	A rainbow

1) It comes in a bottle or tube. **2)** It can protect you. **3)** Some are stronger than others.	Sun block
1) It can get you in financial trouble. **2)** It is made of plastic. **3)** Most grown-ups have one.	A credit card
1) It is placed in the corner of something. **2)** It is sticky. **3)** It travels to many places.	A stamp
1) It can be found inside something. **2)** It can move quickly. **3)** It can get you in trouble.	Your tongue
1) It has a funny looking nose. **2)** It has an unusual diet. **3)** It is a compound word.	An anteater

1) It is shaped like a finger. 2) It is surrounded by water on three sides. 3) You can't find one in Idaho.	A peninsula
1) It usually has wheels. 2) People get mad if it gets lost. 3) It can travel long distances.	A suitcase
1) It needs to be fed. 2) It measures time. 3) It is found outside.	A parking meter
1) It can be found in a vending machine. 2) It's salty and crunchy. 3) It costs less than $5.00.	A package of pretzels
1) It's smaller than a golf ball. 2) You can buy one from a machine. 3) It comes in different colors.	A gumball

1) It is found in many recipes. **2)** It is not round. **3)** It can come in a carton.	An egg
1) It's something you often lose. **2)** It can be found in a purse. **3)** It has four sides.	A wallet
1) It's usually used to improve your appearance. **2)** It will fit in a suitcase. **3)** It needs electricity.	A hair dryer
1) It comes in different shapes. **2)** It comes in a jar or a bottle. **3)** It usually comes with instructions.	A pill
1) It has dates on it. **2)** It can be found in a classroom. **3)** It existed 100 years ago.	A calendar

1) It's long and skinny. **2)** You can break it in half. **3)** It can bend after you cook it.	Spaghetti
1) It usually has a ring. **2)** It is soothing. **3)** Grown-ups don't need one.	A pacifier
1) It is the theme of a holiday. **2)** It can be broken. **3)** It never misses a beat.	A heart
1) It is usually three feet off the ground. **2)** It is usually round. **3)** It is attached to something else.	A door knob
1) Sometimes it flies. **2)** Sometimes it drags. **3)** Sometimes it runs out.	Time

1) It requires more than one person. **2)** It has two handles. **3)** An elephant and a mouse cannot use it together.	A see-saw
1) It would ruin a diet. **2)** It comes in a box. **3)** It can be squished easily.	A doughnut
1) It needs to be maintained. **2)** It's expensive to own. **3)** It's capable of misbehaving.	A horse
1) It's made of wood. **2)** It's hollow inside. **3)** You hope you won't be needing one soon.	A casket
1) Jewelry is made for it. **2)** It has no bones inside. **3)** It comes in a pair.	An earlobe

1) It has an odor. 2) Its price goes up and down. 3) It is flammable.	Gasoline
1) It's very tall. 2) It represents something. 3) It is on an island.	Statue of Liberty
1) It goes in and out of something. 2) It can be metal, plastic or wood. 3) It will not break if you drop it.	A spoon.
1) You would not want to live there. 2) Sometimes people come to visit. 3) It involves spending time.	Jail
1) It's usually made of wood. 2) It has two sharp points. 3) It can be broken in half.	A toothpick

1) You shouldn't give them to a baby. **2)** They cannot cut steak. **3)** They can open and close.	Scissors
1) It opens and closes. **2)** It can have stripes or polka dots. **3)** You don't need it everyday.	An umbrella
1) It helps keep you organized. **2)** It can come in different sizes and colors. **3)** It can be used more than once.	A paper clip
1) It's made of plastic. **2)** It belongs in one room of the house. **3)** It can be thrown away.	A toothbrush
1) You can put your hand in it. **2)** It can have a hole in it. **3)** It can be washed.	A pocket

1) It can light up. 2) It can help you write a story. 3) It can be creative.	Your imagination
1) You wouldn't want to sleep with it. 2) You can't stuff it in a mailbox. 3) It waddles slowly.	A porcupine
1) It makes a noise. 2) It requires two hands. 3) Babies can do it.	Clapping
1) It swims in the ocean. 2) You can buy it in a can. 3) It makes a delicious sandwich.	Tuna fish
1) You cannot see them. 2) They can be counted. 3) They can be burned.	Calories

1) It has two ends.

2) It is used for grooming.

3) You should not use it while driving.

A Q-tip

1) It has a storage compartment.

2) It comes in different sizes.

3) It is only native to one country.

A kangaroo

1) It can grow.

2) It can be cut.

3) It can be painted.

A fingernail

1) They can be made of plastic or wood.

2) They come in a pair.

3) They require practice.

A pair of chopsticks

1) Everybody has them.

2) They sometimes change over time.

3) You can read one in a newspaper.

An opinion

1) It can grab something. **2)** You shouldn't use it while driving. **3)** It can improve your appearance.	A pair of tweezers
1) It is named after an animal. **2)** It can slide and roll. **3)** It controls something else.	A computer mouse
1) It is long and pointy. **2)** It can drip. **3)** It hangs on something.	An icicle
1) It is a compound word. **2)** It has spots. **3)** People like to see them.	A ladybug
1) It is often considered romantic. **2)** It gets smaller when you use it. **3)** It can roll.	A candle

1) It should only be used one way. **2)** You'll be in trouble if you don't. **3)** It cannot fit inside a house.	A one way street
1) People feel happy when you give them one. **2)** It can be paid, yet costs nothing. **3)** They come in all varieties.	A compliment
1) It can be found inside or outside. **2)** It can pinch you. **3)** It was used more often years ago.	A clothespin
1) It can protect a part of your body. **2)** It existed 100 years ago. **3)** It is bumpy.	A thimble
1) Sometimes it could be a teddy bear. **2)** Sometimes it could be a baseball cap **3)** Or perhaps a pretty shell.	A souvenir

1) It can only be used in water. **2)** It requires practice. **3)** It is recreational.	A surfboard
1) It carries cars. **2)** It can go from one place to another. **3)** It requires a ticket.	A ferry boat
1) Ants like them. **2)** They have a lid. **3)** They have a handle.	A picnic basket
1) It is placed under something. **2)** It can be a liquid or a solid. **3)** It can go in a suitcase.	A deodorant
1) It must be obeyed. **2)** It is found on the side of a road. **3)** It is made of metal.	A speed limit sign.

1) It doesn't like being upside down. **2)** Most of the time, it can't win a race. **3)** It can hide.	A tortoise
1) It has a lid. **2)** It can be picked up. **3)** Neighbors don't like to see it.	A dumpster
1) It can pop up at anytime. **2)** Some people have more than one. **3)** It can ruin a prom.	A pimple
1) It can have four sides. **2)** It can have three sides. **3)** Some people should use it more often.	A napkin
1) It can be found between your toes. **2)** It can be found in your bellybutton. **3)** People wonder where it comes from.	Lint

1) It can brighten your day. **2)** It needs to be brushed. **3)** It can be contagious.	A smile
1) It is very tall and skinny. **2)** It has a beacon. **3)** People can climb up inside it.	A lighthouse
1) You wear special shoes to play it **2)** You wouldn't want to drop it on your toe. **3)** It is loud but fun.	A bowling ball
1) A candy bar was named after it. **2)** Part of its name is a dairy product. **3)** It can be seen on a dark night.	The Milky Way
1) It is stationary. **2)** It serves a purpose. **3)** It is stuffed with straw.	A scarecrow

1) It's usually done two at a time. **2)** It happens quite often. **3)** It is necessary.	Blinking
1) People are not glad to see them. **2)** They cannot be ignored. **3)** They are flat.	Bills
1) You can stuff it. **2)** It is flat. **3)** It can travel.	An envelope
1) It is produced constantly. **2)** It can be used as a weapon. **3)** Everybody has some.	Saliva
1) It can be used by a nurse. **2)** It can be used by meteorologists. **3)** It was invented in 1714.	A thermometer

1) It comes in different shapes and sizes. **2)** It has moving parts. **3)** It requires a covering.	Your body
1) It is not real. **2)** It can be pleasant or frightening. **3)** It may or may not be remembered.	A dream
1) It can be found in many foods. **2)** Some people don't approve of it. **3)** It didn't exist 100 years ago.	Artificial flavoring
1) It is wrapped. **2)** It can be found inside something. **3)** It is very old.	A mummy
1) It can float. **2)** It travels to certain sporting events. **3)** It can have advertising on it.	A blimp

1) It is refreshing. 2) Most hotels have one. 3) It can help people exercise.	A pool
1) All rooms have them. 2) Sometimes children are sent there. 3) It is not curved.	A corner
1) It has layers. 2) It does not require a fork. 3) Millions are sold.	A cheeseburger
1) It is not solid. 2) It should be avoided. 3) Things can disappear in it.	Quicksand
1) You are one of its members. 2) They come in different sizes. 3) They can drive you crazy.	Your family

1) You can choose what goes inside it. 2) It needs to be flipped. 3) It can be cooked quickly.	An omelet
1) People can look at it. 2) It can be found on a pond. 3) It can be found in a shop window.	A reflection
1) Some can last a long time. 2) Some people have had more than one. 3) It requires a license.	A marriage
1) Some people keep it. 2) Other people let it out of the bag. 3) It contains information.	A secret
1) It is interesting to hear about it. 2) Neighbors talk about it. 3) It is not something you would want.	A scandal

1) It has small items inside. **2)** Sometimes you can't see it. **3)** It can be found at a party.	A piñata
1) They can be shared. **2)** They can be kept to ourselves. **3)** Sometimes they're deep.	Thoughts
1) It takes practice. **2)** It has moving parts. **3)** Boys don't do them.	Cartwheels
1) Many buildings have them. **2)** It has buttons to push. **3)** It helps people to communicate.	An intercom
1) You can pump it. **2)** It can be found on a desk. **3)** It kills germs.	Hand sanitizer

1) It can be high or low. 2) It can clog something. 3) It can be measured.	Cholesterol
1) They are at least one day old. 2) Some people avoid them. 3) They come in a container.	Leftovers
1) They are usually black and white. 2) You can toss them. 3) They tell you how to move.	Dice
1) It can be heard in a courtroom. 2) Sometimes it's hard to admit. 3) It should always be told.	The truth
1) It is used for grooming. 2) It can fit in tight spaces. 3) Cavemen did not have any.	Dental Floss

1) There are many kinds. **2)** It is helpful to people. **3)** Everyone thinks theirs is the true choice.	Religion
1) It can be felt within the body. **2)** People wish it would go away. **3)** People complain about it.	Pain
1) It is necessary to have it. **2)** Sometimes you lose it. **3)** You have to pay for it.	Electricity
1) Sometimes you lose it. **2)** It can be explosive. **3)** It can get you in trouble.	Your temper
1) People don't shed them every day. **2)** They are very small. **3)** They can roll.	Tears

1) It can make you feel good. 2) It can hurt you. 3) We all wish we had more of this feeling.	Love
1) People express it in different ways. 2) It makes them feel good. 3) You should do it everyday.	Laughter
1) Exercise can help you manage it. 2) People worry about it. 3) It can be measured.	Weight
1) It is unexpected. 2) It can be destructive. 3) It happens in certain places.	An earthquake
1) People make them. 2) There are many kinds. 3) Part of a chicken is named after it.	A wish

1) It can be soft or loud. **2)** It can be high or low. **3)** Sometimes you lose it temporarily.	A voice
1) Some you can sit on. **2)** Some you push. **3)** It can help you earn money.	A lawnmower
1) You can hold it in your lap. **2)** It has moving parts. **3)** It can perform.	A ventriloquist dummy
1) Some people have a dangerous allergy to it. **2)** It can be found at a baseball game. **3)** You can't give it to a baby.	A peanut
1) It is usually served in the morning. **2)** It goes on top of something. **3)** You can squeeze it or pour it.	Maple syrup

1) There is a famous one named Tom. **2)** They usually come in a pair. **3)** They are not very useful by themselves.	A thumb
1) It has sections. **2)** It can be decorated. **3)** Its appearance can change over time.	A snowman
1) It can be carved like a whale. **2)** It can be carved like a basket. **3)** Part of it is fun to spit.	A watermelon
1) You can read it. **2)** You can fold it. **3)** It represents something.	A map
1) It makes a job easier. **2)** It is only used during one season. **3)** Nobody has one in Florida.	A snow blower

1) It can be grown. **2)** It can be eaten. **3)** It is hard to lift.	A bale of hay
1) It is small. **2)** It requires a battery. **3)** It is helpful to some people.	A hearing aid
1) It can be shaped like a ring. **2)** It can roll. **3)** It can make you cry.	An onion
1) Some people go there every week. **2)** It is a good idea to bring a book. **3)** It requires coins.	A Laundromat
1) It can only be found outside. **2)** It is rarely used. **3)** It requires a wrench to open.	A fire hydrant

1) It can measure something. **2)** It can make you cry. **3)** People step on it.	A scale
1) We look at it everyday. **2)** It is usually mounted on the wall. **3)** It existed 100 years ago.	A clock
1) It is seen at celebrations. **2)** It can make you talk funny. **3)** It is easily lost.	A helium balloon
1) It is usually kept in the kitchen. **2)** It has a handle. **3)** It is used for one purpose.	An ice cream scoop
1) Everybody has them. **2)** Nobody wants them. **3)** You should keep yours to yourself.	Germs

1) It has two syllables. **2)** It has a funny name. **3)** Most people have never seen one.	An aardvark
1) It is usually pink or blue. **2)** It is usually found in fun places. **3)** It does not require a fork.	Cotton candy
1) It can hang on a wall. **2)** It can catch something. **3)** It is not used in the city.	A lasso
1) It can be used in an art project. **2)** It can be boiled. **3)** Part of its name is a body part.	Elbow macaroni
1) It can be used in an art project. **2)** It can be used at a hospital. **3)** You can't eat it.	A cotton ball

1) Some are kept. **2)** Some are broken. **3)** Some are a secret.	A promise
1) It can be positive or negative. **2)** Sometimes it has a picture on it. **3)** It is attracted to something.	A magnet
1) Some are stronger than others. **2)** People get mad if they lose one. **3)** They require a prescription.	Contact lenses
1) Children love it when they don't have any. **2)** It is easy to forget. **3)** Sometimes your dog eats it.	Homework
1) They wear reflective clothing **2)** They don't work year round. **3)** They do not receive a high salary.	A school crossing guard

1) It's usually your fault if you get one. **2)** Some people have received more than one. **3)** A turtle can't get one.	A speeding ticket
1) You can surf on it. **2)** It can be dangerous. **3)** It can take you to many interesting sites.	The Internet
1) It can look like a duck. **2)** It can look like a whale. **3)** It can look like a fish.	An Inflatable float
1) It can pull something. **2)** It is usually expensive to own one. **3)** It needs to be guided.	A motorboat
1) Only certain people can fit inside it. **2)** It can be bought new or used. **3)** It has bars.	A crib

1) It was invented in 1913. **2)** It makes a noise when it is moving. **3)** It can be replaced if it breaks.	A zipper
1) It can cause arguments. **2)** It can be used to help other people. **3)** It is usually found inside something.	Money
1) It will break if you drop it. **2)** It can be empty or full. **3)** It can't oink.	A piggy bank
1) Part of its name is a language. **2)** It has holes in it. **3)** It can grow moldy.	An English muffin
1) It can run. **2)** It can drip. **3)** It can blow.	A nose

1) They can cling to someone.

2) They can misbehave.

3) They can grow.

A toddler

1) It has a funny looking nose.

2) It can be a cute stuffed animal.

3) Part of it looks like a tree branch.

A moose

1) Some have more information than others.

2) It changes over time.

3) A famous scarecrow wished he had one.

A brain

1) It takes a long time for one to be created.

2) Some are bigger than others.

3) It is valuable.

A diamond

1) It can be tiny.

2) It can be molded.

3) It is hard to walk on.

Sand

1) Different people have lived there. **2)** It is protected. **3)** It has a rose garden.	The White House
1) It can sway in the wind. **2)** A famous one was twins. **3)** It cannot be seen in the country.	A skyscraper
1) It is not connected to anything. **2)** You can't get there by car or train. **3)** Nantucket is one.	An island
1) It is made from thread. **2)** It can be repaired. **3)** It is sticky.	A spider web
1) It cannot moo. **2)** It can perform. **3)** You cannot iron out its wrinkles.	An elephant

1) It does not do well in hurricanes. **2)** It usually has a destination. **3)** It would ruin a diet.	A cruise ship
1) It can be a jam but not a jelly. **2)** People avoid it. **3)** It is frustrating.	A traffic jam
1) It is a mixture. **2)** It can be dressed. **3)** It is fresh and crisp.	A salad
1) It can be found at a hotel. **2)** It is warm and bubbly. **3)** It has a funny name.	A Jacuzzi
1) You can throw something at other people. **2)** Nobody gets hurt. **3)** It feels refreshing.	A water balloon fight

1) It has something inside. **2)** You can crack it open. **3)** It can be buried.	A walnut
1) It is part of an elephant. **2)** It is part of a car. **3)** It rhymes with skunk.	A trunk
1) It can submerge. **2)** It can travel long distances. **3)** It is crowded inside.	A submarine
1) It is a compound word. **2)** You can find it at a movie theater. **3)** It can get stuck between your teeth.	Popcorn
1) Part of its name is a language. **2)** It is square. **3)** It needs to be flipped.	French toast

1) It can echo. **2)** People travel to see it. **3)** You can see one on a postcard.	A canyon
1) It is necessary for some vacations. **2)** Sometimes it arrives late. **3)** Some people are afraid of it.	An airplane.
1) People enjoy looking at it. **2)** Sometimes you can see one in a restaurant. **3)** It needs to be kept clean.	An aquarium
1) Some people dye it purple. **2)** Some people shave it off. **3)** Some people wish they had more.	Hair
1) It is used for special occasions. **2)** Some are longer than others. **3)** It is always expensive.	A limousine

1) It usually looks blue. **2)** It has a liquid inside. **3)** It is long and skinny.	A vein
1) It needs to be drilled. **2)** It is not something you would want. **3)** It can be prevented.	A cavity
1) It tastes good with a doughnut. **2)** Some people buy it everyday. **3)** Some people are grouchy if they don't get some.	A cup of coffee
1) Rabbits like it. **2)** It usually has a fence. **3)** It can help you be healthy.	A garden
1) This person can be young or old. **2)** Sometimes we give them a party. **3)** They can make us proud.	A student

1) It can be helpful. **2)** It can be destructive. **3)** It can be found inside or outside.	A fire
1) It can light up. **2)** It can be seen at night. **3)** It can be caught in a jar.	A firefly
1) It does not wear a collar. **2)** It cannot bark. **3)** It does not need to be walked.	A hotdog
1) It has no students. **2)** It has no teachers. **3)** It never graduates.	A school of fish.
1) You cannot climb it. **2)** It has no snow on top. **3)** No animals live there.	A mountain of laundry

1) It is not good for making shoes. **2)** It can be liquid or solid. **3)** You can make a footprint in it.	Cement
1) A girl named Dorothy traveled inside one. **2)** Her dog, Toto did, too. **3)** It brought them down safely.	A tornado
1) Some are silver, some are gold. **2)** It's usually romantic. **3)** A husband will be in the doghouse If he forgets it.	An anniversary
1) Visitors use it. **2)** It makes a sound. **3)** Sometimes it is broken.	A doorbell
1) It is only used once. **2)** It comes in a wrapper. **3)** It is sticky.	A band-aid

1) Drivers can do it. **2)** Part of its name is an alphabet letter. **3)** You can't do it on the highway.	A U-turn
1) It gets nervous in November. **2)** It can be stuffed. **3)** You can ask for the drumstick.	A turkey
1) It can be worn by a motorcyclist. **2)** It can be worn by a horseback rider. **3)** It can be worn by a football player.	A helmet
1) It is connected to something else. **2)** It can growl. **3)** Some are bigger than others.	A stomach
1) It is usually found on the ceiling. **2)** It usually requires a battery. **3)** It can save lives.	A smoke detector

1) It has a funny shape. **2)** It doesn't last forever. **3)** You can't take it camping.	A light bulb
1) It has keys. **2)** It's not easily moved. **3)** It requires two hands.	A piano
1) It's a healthy food. **2)** It's curved. **3)** It can be green or yellow.	A banana
1) It can be carved. **2)** It can be baked in a pie. **3)** You can eat its seeds.	A pumpkin
1) It can crash. **2)** It can carry people. **3)** It can only be found at the beach or a water park.	A wave

1) It has a funny shape. **2)** It can live in a harsh habitat. **3)** Sometimes it can be stubborn.	A camel
1) It is usually not found in the city. **2)** It makes a loud noise. **3)** Part of it can be squeezed.	A cow
1) It usually goes inside something else. **2)** It has four sides. **3)** It can be folded.	A dollar
1) It usually is found outside. **2)** It is tied to something. **3)** It's not used as often as in the past.	A clothes line
1) Sometimes it is hard to get rid of them. **2)** They are annoying. **3)** Their cause is unknown.	Hiccups

1) It can be used more than once. **2)** It comes in different colors. **3)** It is worn on the body.	A parachute
1) It's soft. **2)** You take it camping. **3)** You can stuff it in your mouth.	A marshmallow
1) It can be rolled up. **2)** Sometimes a puppy uses it. **3)** It can be brought on a train.	A newspaper
1) People look forward to it. **2)** It can be cheap or expensive. **3)** Children usually have more than grown-ups.	A Vacation
1) It usually lasts 15 minutes. **2)** Children feel sad when it is over. **3)** It is busy like a bee hive.	Recess

1) It can fall to the ground. 2) It is shiny like a new penny. 3) It can be roasted.	A chestnut
1) Many tourists came to see it. 2) It had a famous nickname. 3) One morning people looked up and it was gone.	The Old Man in the Mountain
1) Only certain animals wear one. 2) It can be adjusted. 3) It can be removed.	A collar
1) It can only be seen under a microscope. 2) It can divide itself. 3) It requires water to live.	An amoeba
1) It can fit in a pocket. 2) It can vibrate. 3) It can flip open.	A cell phone

1) It cannot meow. **2)** It cannot purr. **3)** It cannot scratch.	A dust kitty
1) It is a compound word. **2)** It is a stool but you can't sit on it. **3)** It is shaped like an umbrella.	A toadstool
1) It can be found on a necklace. **2)** It takes a long time for one to form. **3)** It is created inside a shell.	A pearl
1) It can be spoken or written. **2)** It usually has a plot. **3)** It can unfold.	A story
1) It can sing songs. **2)** It can migrate. **3)** It can consume a million calories a day.	A whale

1) It can be avoided. **2)** It can peel. **3)** It usually happens outside.	A sunburn
1) People enjoy talking about it. **2)** Sometimes it causes problems. **3)** It can change from day to day.	The weather
1) You can squeeze it. **2)** It is usually found in the kitchen. **3)** It has holes in it.	A sponge
1) It has 26 members. **2)** It can make many combinations. **3)** There is a song about it.	The alphabet
1) Children are taught where to put it. **2)** It belongs at the end of something. **3)** It is very small.	A period

1) People giggle if you say its name. **2)** Some are more comfortable than others. **3)** It is usually hidden.	Underwear
1) You can walk across it. **2)** Different events can take place there. **3)** It usually has a curtain.	A stage
1) It can be black, blue or purple. **2)** It fades over time. **3)** It does not require a band-aid.	A bruise
1) A rooster knows when it comes. **2)** It happens every day. **3)** It can be seen in the eastern sky.	A sunrise
1) It is popular at Halloween. **2)** 4 of its 8 letters spell a boy's name. **3)** It rhymes with "stickers."	Snickers

1) It is pretend. **2)** It can be invisible. **3)** It can float.	A ghost
1) It can float. **2)** It can sting. **3)** It is a compound word.	A jellyfish
1) Some are funnier than others. **2)** People share them. **3)** They have a punch line.	A joke
1) It can improve your mood. **2)** You can dance to it. **3)** You can listen to it in the car.	Music
1) It can get tired. **2)** It can be strengthened. **3)** Superman's were impressive.	A muscle

1) It can be found in a school hallway. **2)** It can be decorated. **3)** It changes with the seasons.	A bulletin board
1) You can squeeze it. **2)** You can leave the cap off. **3)** It is refreshing.	A tube of toothpaste
1) It can help you study. **2)** It comes in fluorescent colors. **3)** It cannot be erased.	A highlighter
1) It requires balance to use one. **2)** It can only be used by one person. **3)** It was invented in 1919.	A pogo stick
1) Most desks have one. **2)** It needs to be refilled. **3)** It helps keep us organized.	A stapler

1) It is usually found in a backyard. **2)** It is usually circular. **3)** A kangaroo would be good at it.	A trampoline
1) It was invented in 1962. **2)** It requires no hands. **3)** It is good exercise.	A hula hoop
1) It has no brakes. **2)** It requires no hands. **3)** You can do stunts with it.	A skateboard
1) It can be blocked. **2)** It can be passed. **3)** It can score.	A soccer ball
1) It can be seen on Oct 31st. **2)** It is not used for sweeping. **3)** It is a form of transportation.	A witch's broomstick

1) It can be romantic. **2)** It happens everyday. **3)** It can be seen in the western sky.	A sunset
1) They are always found together. **2)** They are black and white. **3)** One of them can make you sneeze.	Salt and pepper shakers
1) They are black and white. **2)** They can be lined up. **3)** They can be knocked over.	Dominoes
1) Some drive faster than others. **2)** You can whistle to catch one. **3)** You must pay for it.	A taxi
1) Some are shaped like an animal. **2)** Some have a silver lining. **3)** Some can turn pretty colors at sunset.	Clouds

1) Some policemen have one. **2)** It is loud. **3)** It can fit in your pocket.	A whistle
1) Ducks like it. **2)** It provides drinking water. **3)** It can ruin a parade.	Rain
1) It is usually green. **2)** It can hang from a thread. **3)** It is fun to watch.	An inchworm
1) It is polite to use one. **2)** It can be stacked. **3)** It protects something.	A coaster
1) You can drop it. **2)** You can take it. **3)** It rhymes with "lint".	A hint

1) They are found inside something. **2)** They can be removed. **3)** They can be seen in a smile.	Dentures
1) It happens on the same date every year. **2)** It is celebrated at night. **3)** Some people throw a party for it.	Halloween
1) She wishes to be human. **2)** Her friends are sea creatures. **3)** She doesn't have legs.	A mermaid
1) It is a compound word. **2)** It usually can't be postponed. **3)** It's not really dead.	A deadline
1) It is a compound word. **2)** It is flat. **3)** It is placed between something.	A bookmark

1) It has a funny name. **2)** It can be octagonal or square. **3)** You can build one in your backyard.	A gazebo
1) It cannot move sideways. **2)** It comes when it is called. **3)** It can be empty or full.	An elevator
1) This person is behind you. **2)** They are never welcome. **3)** You can see them in the mirror.	A tailgater
1) It does not belong in the house. **2)** You can make pies with it. **3)** It cannot be found in the desert.	Mud
1) It is transparent. **2)** It can predict the future. **3)** Witches use them.	A crystal ball

1) It comes in a box. **2)** It can be struck. **3)** It can be taken on a camping trip.	A matchstick
1) You can throw it. **2)** It is colorful. **3)** It can get stuck in your hair.	Confetti
1) It offers many choices. **2)** It can ruin a diet. **3)** It is a french word.	A buffet
1) It can be found on the back of a car. **2)** It comes in a pair. **3)** It can blink.	A directional
1) It is helpful to a driver. **2)** It is attached to the windshield. **3)** It can be adjusted.	A rear view mirror

1) It is worn on the body. **2)** It is long and skinny. **3)** It has a knot.	A necktie
1) It can hang from a branch. **2)** It has seeds inside. **3)** Its visitors have feathers.	A bird feeder
1) It can be found in a backyard. **2)** It is filled with water. **3)** Its visitors take a bath.	A bird bath
1) It comes in a can. **2)** It is light and fluffy. **3)** It is a dairy product.	Whipped cream
1) It is very hungry. **2)** It moves very slowly. **3)** It can transform itself.	A caterpillar

1) It is rectangular. **2)** People hand them out. **3)** It has personal information.	A business card
1) It usually has a lock and key. **2)** It can be kept in a hidden location. **3)** It is very private.	A diary
1) It has a funny name. **2)** It has three syllables. **3)** You won't find one at the "zu."	A zucchini
1) Witches have them. **2)** Toads have them. **3)** It rhymes with quart.	A wart
1) They are full of hot air. **2)** They can talk out of two sides of their mouth. **3)** They can change their tune.	A politician

1) It is made with three ingredients. **2)** One of them is roasted and gooey. **3)** The other two are square and flat.	A smore
1) You can't sleep there. **2)** It is fragrant. **3)** It needs to be tended.	A flower bed
1) It is not used on Sundays. **2)** It is usually shaped like a loaf of bread. **3)** Sometimes it gets buried in the snow.	A mailbox
1) It is done horizontally. **2)** It can be counted. **3)** It can make you stronger.	A push-up
1) It requires two people. **2)** It cannot oink. **3)** It looks silly.	A piggy back ride

1) You can pound on its head. **2)** It won't get mad. **3)** It is used in carpentry.	A nail
1) It is placed inside things. **2)** It can grow weak. **3)** It can be replaced.	A battery
1) It is done horizontally. **2)** It is usually refreshing. **3)** A dream may happen.	Sleeping
1) It could be a rhumba or a cha-cha. **2)** It can be done with one, two or more people. **3)** It is good exercise.	Dancing
1) It is constructed by a busy animal. **2)** It is done near water. **3)** It is impressive.	A beaver dam

1) It is done with the hands. **2)** It is messy but fun. **3)** You usually wear a smock.	Finger painting
1) It usually requires a bus. **2)** It is a special event. **3)** It requires chaperones.	A field trip
1) Scuba divers like to visit it. **2)** It is colorful. **3)** It is endangered.	A coral reef
1) Kids love it. **2)** Parents hate it. **3)** They say 'yes' anyway.	A sleepover
1) It can be found in a classroom. **2)** It can be solved. **3)** It can make you smarter.	A riddle

1) It can fall to the ground. **2)** It can pile up. **3)** It can be measured.	Snow
1) Peter Pan lost his temporarily. **2)** It follows you around. **3)** It cannot be seen in the shade.	A shadow
1) No one knows how it gets started. **2)** It can be spread around. **3)** It may or may not be true.	A rumor
1) It has a pit inside. **2)** It has a rough skin. **3)** It has four syllables.	An avocado

RIDDLE INDEX

sand 39
scale 34
scandal 26
scarecrow 22
school crossing guard 36
school of fish 45
scissors 15
secret 26
see-saw 13
shadow 68
skateboard 57
sleeping 66
sleepover 67
skyscraper 40
smile 22
smoke detector 47
smore 65
Snickers 54
snow 68
snow blower 32
snowman 32
soccer ball 57
souvenir 19
spaghetti 12
speeding ticket 37
speed limit sign 20
spider web 40
sponge 53
spoon 14
stage 54
stamp 9
stapler 56
Statue of Liberty 14
stomach 47

story 52
student 44
submarine 42
suitcase 10
sun block 9
sunburn 53
sunrise 54
sunset 58
surfboard 20

tailgater 61
tattoo 8
taxi 58
tears 29
thermometer 23
thimble 19
thoughts 27
thumb 32
time 12
toadstool 52
toddler 39
toothbrush 15
toothpick 14
tornado 46
tortoise 21
traffic jam 41
trampoline 57
trunk 42
truth 28
tube of toothpaste 56
tunafish 16
turkey 47

u-turn 47

umbrella 15
underwear 54

vacation 50
vein 44
ventriloquist dummy 31
voice 31

wallet 11
walnut 42
water balloon fight 41
watermelon 32
wave 48
weather 53
wedding 6
wart 64
weight 30
whale 52
whipped cream 63
whistle 59
white house 40
wish 30
witch's broomstick 57
wrinkles 6

your age 6
your body 24
your family 25
your imagination 16
your temper 24
your tongue 9

zipper 38
zucchini 64

www.ingramcontent.com/pod-product-compliance
Lightning Source LLC
Chambersburg PA
CBHW080936040426
42443CB00015B/3441